DEDICATED TO
PROPHET MUHAMMAD
(PEACE BE UPON HIM),
THE GREATEST MUSLIM
TO HAVE EVER LIVED

IN THE NAME OF ALLAH (SWT), THE KIND, THE MERCIFUL

PUBLISHED BY SUN BEHIND THE CLOUD PUBLICATIONS LTD
PO BOX 15889, BIRMINGHAM, B16 6NZ

THIS EDITION FIRST PUBLISHED IN 2018
© COPYRIGHT ZAINAB MERCHANT 2018
ILLUSTRATIONS BY SHIELA ALEJANDRO

ALL RIGHTS RESERVED. NO PART OF THIS PUBLICATION MAY BE REPRODUCED BY ANY MEANS WITHOUT THE EXPRESS PERMISSION OF THE PUBLISHER.

ISBN (HARDBACK): 978-1-908110-52-7
ISBN (PAPERBACK): 978-1-908110-56-5
ISBN (EBOOK): 978-1-908110-53-4

A CIP CATALOGUE RECORD OF THIS BOOK IS AVAILABLE FROM THE BRITISH LIBRARY.

WWW.SUNBEHINDTHECLOUD.COM
INFO@SUNBEHINDTHECLOUD.COM

TO BE A MUSLIM

WRITTEN BY
ZAINAB MERCHANT

TO BE LOVING AND KIND JUST LIKE HIM,
NOT ANGRY OR SELFISH OR GROUCHY OR GRIM

SO WITH A WARM AND FRIENDLY CHEERFUL SMILE,
I CARE FOR MY NEIGHBOURS WITH A PROPHETIC LIFESTYLE

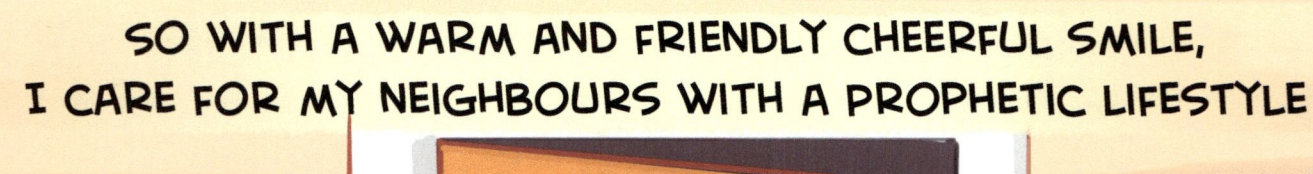

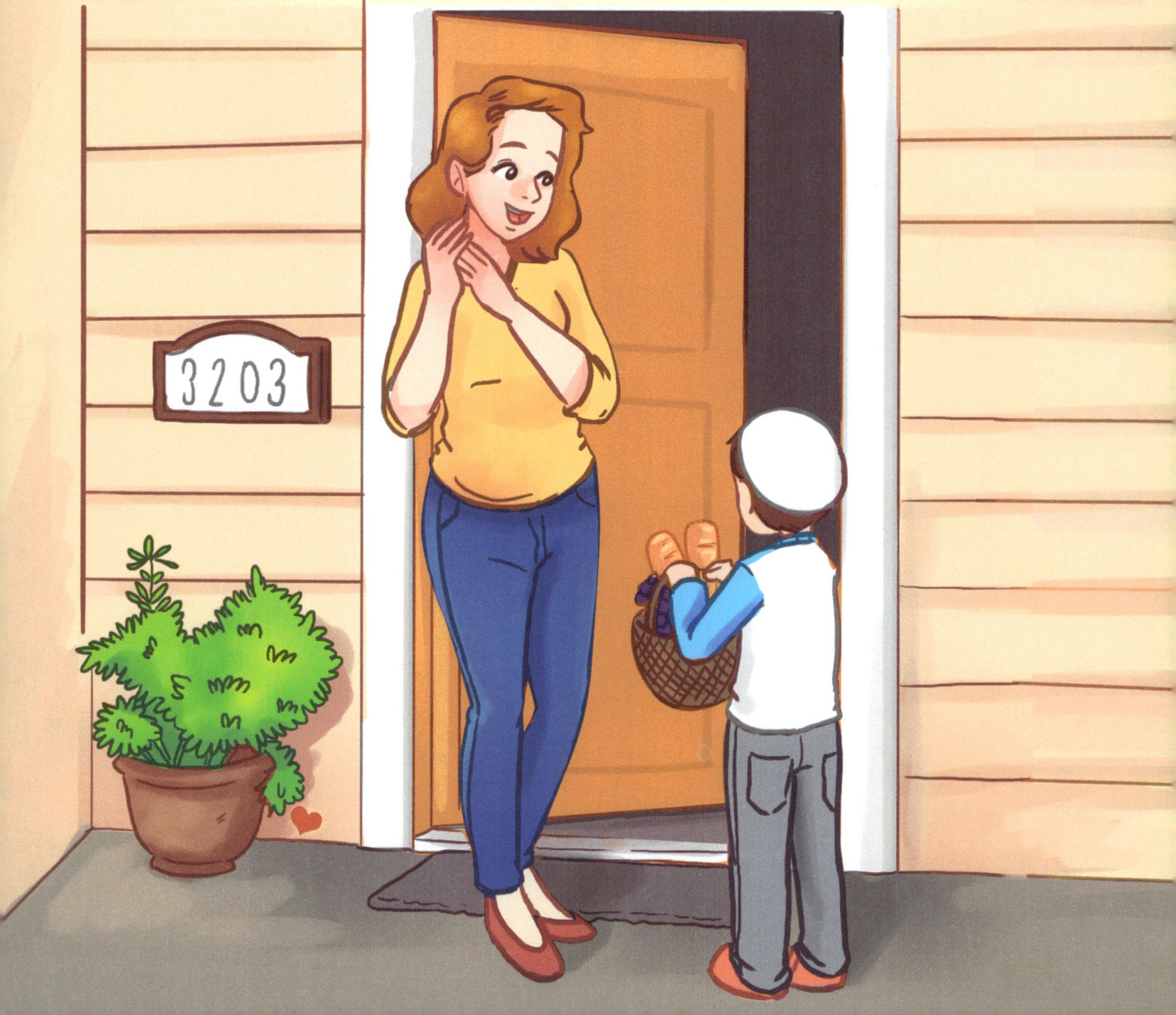

I FOLLOW THE FOOTSTEPS OF THOSE SENT TO GUIDE,
SUCH AS MUHAMMAD, JESUS, AND MOSES –
MY LIGHT AND PRIDE

I REFLECT AND RECHARGE FIVE TIMES A DAY, STOPPING ON TIME, SO THAT I CAN PRAY

BEHIND THE BOOK: IN A WESTERN SOCIETY THAT IS RICH IN CULTURE AND DIVERSE IN FAITH, TO BE PROUD OF ONE'S ISLAMIC IDENTITY IS PARAMOUNT IN REPRESENTING ITS TRUE ETHICS AND MORALS. THIS BOOK SEEKS TO ENCOURAGE YOUNG MINDS AND HEARTS TO STRIVE TO BE SINCERE MUSLIMS; FOLLOW THE PILLARS OF ISLAM; GRASP THE MEANING OF THE QURAN AND SUNNAH; UNDERSTAND THEIR UNLIMITED POTENTIALS, AND NURTURE THEIR GOOD CHARACTERS.

ZAINAB MERCHANT IS A WRITER, JOURNALIST AND MOTHER OF THREE, ALL OF WHICH HAVE CONTRIBUTED TO HER PERSPECTIVE THAT MUSLIM VOICES ARE ESSENTIAL IN THE WORLD TODAY! SHE IS THE AUTHOR OF PRINCESS SIYANA'S PEN, AND UPCOMING TITLES BINOCULAR MAN AND SUPER POWER PRAYER – WHICH FOCUS ON HIGHLIGHTING THE TRUE VALUES OF ISLAM AND ITS TEACHINGS. ZAINAB STUDIES JOURNALISM AND INTERNATIONAL SECURITY AT HARVARD UNIVERSITY AND SEEKS TO PURSUE HER CURRENT PASSION IN ANIMATION AND SERVING UNDER-REPRESENTED VOICES CREATIVELY.

ACKNOWLEDGEMENTS: TO MY LORD, FOR WILLING THIS BOOK INTO FRUITION. TO THE HOLY PROPHET (PBUH) AND HIS FAMILY FOR THEIR EXAMPLE THAT CONTINUES TO GUIDE THE WAY. TO MY PARENTS, HUSBAND AND FAMILY, FOR THEIR UNREQUITED SUPPORT. TO MY PUBLISHER TEHSEEN, FOR HER DETERMINATION AND BRILLIANCE. TO MY LATE FATHER ABBAS PARPIA WHOSE PASSING HAS INSPIRED ME TOWARDS GOODNESS, AND TO ALL WHO HAVE FOLLOWED AND ENCOURAGED MY WORK, YOU ARE THE TRUE STARS.

www.ingramcontent.com/pod-product-compliance
Lightning Source LLC
Chambersburg PA
CBHW042252100526
44587CB00002B/113